Guernsey Chronicles

Anita B. Harmon

Guernsey Chronicles

Published by the Actors Mind Press
Actors Mind Professional Development
Rancho Mirage, CA 92270 USA

Original cover design by Andy Harmon © 2018. Based on a photograph of Saints Bay, St Martins, Guernsey, the image was processed in Photoshop. The B&W photograph of the poet and her grandmother that appears on the back cover was taken at Petit Bow, Guernsey around 1952. It is used courtesy of Anita Harmon.

Guernsey Chronicles by Anita Harmon © 2018

ISBN: 978-0-9967608-4-3

Guernsey Chronicles

by

Anita B. Harmon

AFTER THE BOMBING

London 1945

The sky is silent now. Just clouds
to shape-change the hulls of houses
run aground on our street.

Cumulus shadows flow up the stair treads
past a fire place - hung too high on a wall
in a bedroom wallpaper of roses.

In Old Brompton Cemetery
the vibrations of war have shuddered
Victorian skulls out of their mausoleums,
to nest in the sweet peas run wild.

*

The coldest winter on record
since the time of King William

        said my father
so we go to the Odeon -
for the warmth of the crowd, the crowing
Pathe Pictorial cockerel
- our source of news.

We watch women with black lips
crowd to the edge of pavements
waving flags at enormous men
who shake hands and smile

I see man-high heaps of driftwood
cast up by unspeakable storms.
Tree trunks carved by flint waves
flayed to the bone - a wood pile
of men so thin, so naked -
they assume a fundamental aspect
of some other material that might
keep us warm.

*

Mummy likes to go to the posh bombsites
to discuss God who made everything natural
like the Thames, the Sycamore, the Butterfly Bush,
and the Wisteria that has fallen across the ballroom
floor where Douglas Fairbanks Junior used to live.

- where we go to picnic
on the shattered tiles of his conservatory.

There, we consider man-made things
such as railing spikes, blue smashed
medicine bottles, a hob-nailed boot
and his wrought-iron spiral stair
that helixed up into the clouds.

*

My mother and father came apart one day:
You're going on an aero-plane all by yourself

Don't worry Daddy I'll sit in the front
behind Pontius Pilate

Because I knew he was a fair man
because I knew he had to wash his hands

- even though he didn't want to
-even though he didn't want Jesus to die.

Equinox Gale

I take the big golfing umbrella
from out of the hall stand where it
rattles along, next to walking sticks
and other, lesser umbrellas.

I want the Goose-headed black silk
but Granny says: *It's all split darling*
and raps the barometer to prove the point.

Outside the squall goes sideways,
but I am striped in red, yellow, green and blue
so I dare tilt the handle
to get a good look at the sky
and a blast yanks my arms upwards
pulls my toes onto ballerina points

but I daren't hold on
so the brolly spirals over the garden wall
clicks away on its pins, doing cartwheels
as it races toward Icart Point.

War Stories

It was my Grandmother who gave me

the scent of sea-salt and lavender

the call of a gull and the knocking of stones

in the turn of the waves.

Granny's sun is a star

that bobs in her plastic cup

the one that unscrews

from the top of her thermos flask

We have afternoon tea

on top of a German bunker

and I find a bloody napkin

-    a real trophy of war

left by a wounded German soldier.

Put it back darling it's got germs

With Aunty Lois or maybe Aunty Sis

who never married because

all their men died in the Great War.

They tell me how

to pack up my troubles

in my old kit bag and smile, smile,

smile and how I have to say good bye

to Piccadilly and Leicester Square as well.

Their stories of love lost between

iron and concrete, bullets and barbed wire

and the weight they all carried

on the back of a song.

Here I am.

on Granny's lawn with Maggie
my best friend and Jason Granny's cocker spaniel
has just printed his pug-prints across the dew.

We have to go to church where god is boring
but we have to be polite and any way

he wasn't much trouble in those in those days,
only needing us to keep still for an hour or so
every Sunday and watch the stained-glass colors
inch across the hymnals.

*

Elsie's Pleasure

Elsie rings the front door bell in her best felt hat

the one with the brown felt peony

and says in her high voice

Gor Mrs Ashodwn aye I've come to be your 'elp

Granny doubts for a second because Elsie is simple and from the

girls home and she is over forty which is old for a maid

but Granny prayed for help

with old Uncle Ashdown who puts his trousers on

the wrong way round and falls over and anyway

Granny knows God's ways are not our ways.

So I share Elsie's room in the Attic

and she lets me play with the buttons

in her old button box.

On her days off she goes to Grande Roque

to watch the mail boat come in

and I can go too

as long as I don't spoil Elsie's pleasure.

Together we watch the ship do her slow-slow

sideways drift to the dock

while men scurry with rope

and the gulls go ki ki

and Elsie's pleasure is little sparks

that shower us both with pin pricks of joy

as we wave and wave to all the visitors.

Wild Sea Spinach

Aunty Lois is Granny's best friend
and she knows where to find the wild sea-spinach

The three of us go single file
along the shore-line beside the sea
booming its cannons and sure enough

we find it crouched down in a green wheel
out of the wind that flaps our coats
pulls our hair and makes us cry

Aunty Lois says it's more substantial
than garden spinach

so when we boil it later in an old
aluminum pot, it doesn't reduce to nothing

and Granny poaches three eggs
laid by Faith, Hope and Charity

and tips them onto plates of wild sea-spinach
and that is our supper under the wind
still raving inside the kitchen chimney
Aunty Lois, Granny and me.

Tiger Paws

Granny keeps her tiger paws
in the tall-boy by the back door

along with old Wellingtons
badminton rackets and croquet balls
all sewn together by winter spiders.

That naughty German officer!
He cut off the paws and tail when he stole
our tiger skin. But he never found the silver
buried in the greenhouse

A source of satisfaction every lunch time.

I like to push my hands
all the way down to the claws
to sniff their rough striped tiger feel
and the faint charcoal whiff of their burning
in the forest, of that long-ago Indian night.

*

Every Wednesday is market day
so we go to St Peter Port to buy corn
for Faith, Hope and Charity
and bone shaped biscuits for Jason.

We hurry in Granny's hurry-up-trot
to the Iron Monger behind his counter

who keeps his ruler folded up round its brass hinges.
in his top pocket.

Behind us market-day voices -
the clack of heels on the cobble stones
and the high keen of gulls.

Beside us the wet-hay smell of Hessian sacks
rolled back at the top like Frank's shirt sleeves
when he mows our lawn.

Before us rolls of chain and locks and keys
and nails and screws and a box of wooden
wedges for keeping doors open
so we can smell the salt fresh air

12

which Granny says is good for us

and so they can't slam shut in the wind from the sea.

Frank Speaking

Old Mrs Timmer's in a bad way Mrs Ashdown

Frank comes twice a week to do the garden
has his tea-break at eleven o'clock

Yes Frank yes

Drop of rain and that wall's going to come down

Granny in the kitchen flouncing
with her hot pans and pots

Yes Frank yes

You'll be wanting those grapes before long aye

Sipping his mug of tea - speaking his mind

Yes Frank yes

Before they've gone to the mildew I suppose.

Ghosts

I found a book on ghosts that rampaged at night
released from their Victorian bindings by my
need to know all about *The Hanging Judge*
who sentenced everyone to death.

After he died he became a giant rat
in his mahogany study - a noose between his rat teeth

forcing the lonely cyclist
who came in from the storm
to hang himself.

Then there was *The Highway Man's Coat*
that came off its hook if anyone
dared to shelter in the abandoned mansion

the only clue the hungry pathways
it made, as it dragged its stiff and
mildewed skirts through the dust -

and as it reached out of the dark,
boiling empty space, I'd pray
the only help-me prayer I knew

Oh, hear us when we cry to Thee,

For those in peril on the sea!

Best Friends

We listened to the wind in the telegraph lines
as it harped the wires and thrummed
down the pine-tree pole into our ears
pressed to the wood.

This telegraph pole stood outside my best friend's house.
In the smoke-scented evening

one star hung in the sky.

We listened to ships on blue waves
with white gulls and the wind's moan

in their rigging. We saw men in tricorn hats
with flint-stock pistols, felt the yearning
of their masts against winter skies.

I was young then, and my best friend I loved
with all my heart, and her best self
was my best self, and as best friends
we were bound to this wind that spoke to us
and blew we could not know where.

The old house was sold last summer.
On a bright and empty day we see the rooms
have shifted their focus. The walls need paint
- the barn roof caved in. Damp has ruined the go-down
       that still smells of winter apples.

Through the kitchen window washing the last cup
I watch my mother in the garden, picking roses
for the new tenants and I see her age
       in the curve of her bending

But these old granite walls still keep faith
with other days of unspooling cloud
the gong for lunch, the hurry of feet on the stairs
       the marks on the door frame

to record my height from seven to fifteen
and under the place where the table used to be
the ghost of Jason our old Spaniel dog dreams on
- transparent as plankton

That eternal time of childhood's summer

-still set on the south side of the island among fields and lanes, not far from the sea. Maggie and I are still there, walking along the lanes next to hedges of long green grass, primroses and ragged robin. We still gather these flowers and put them into pre-war mustard pots for Granny's desk.

How perfectly lovely darling. Thank you very much Margaret.

Here she still is - doing her letter-writing and household accounts. When the postman comes he will still crunch the gravel first, before his feet clink the shingle by the front door to post the letters. Granny writes letters every day. She has two brothers and two sisters, and friends from school from when she was young. They still write to her of their lives and news - even though everyone is long dead and gone.

Somehow, I inherited my Grandmother's letter opener and I keep it in a tray of pens on my own desk. It came from her brother Arch, who went to live in Canada before World War I. It is in the shape of a mortar trowel and was a free gift from Merchants Insurance Agencies, Ltd., along with the slogan *Build for Safety.*

I suppose we all haunt the objects in our lives, vainly re-defining the smoke of past experience and the time it glowed with the immortal strength of love at first sight.

Let us go down to the sea, Granny said
Let us take our towels and our thermos of tea
go down to where the sea comes in
rolling over and over its edges
We shall find our rock in the un-shedding wind
drink our tea and listen to the gulls calling
'Kind Kind'

We shall look up at their eternal
white flakes wheeling up there in the blue.

The storm is coming, Maggie said. It is forecast.
Let us go to Icart Point and let me show you
how to lie along the gale as it roars
up the granite wall of the cliff.
I shall show you how to stretch your arms wide
lean out over empty space feel the sea-spray fly
and the sea salt sting and you shall see
your wind tears will flow up instead of down.

www.ingramcontent.com/pod-product-compliance
Lightning Source LLC
Chambersburg PA
CBHW032111040426
42449CB00007B/1245